GH00374457

Footsteps from t

Introduction

For visitors new to the Cotswolds there must be a prosaic charm in discovering on the map the villages Upper and Lower Slaughter. In benign simplicity the Saxon place-names allude to 'the valley of the marsh'. The marsh is largely tamed and under manorial rule the agricultural villages have come down the ages to us in tidy homogeneous order, as befits the setting. Throughout England village pairs exist, but few, if any, embody more surely the sense of rural picturesque than the Slaughters.

With the draining of the ancient marsh came the cutting of the mill-race to harness the fall of the River Eye, to power a Saxon mill, first documentary mention of which comes in the Domesday entry of 1086. The present building is founded on a structure dating from the early 1600s and, while there are scant records of its working life as a corn mill, it was last run by four generations of the Wilkins family. Upon the death of Maurice Wilkins in 1958, the mill was sold to the Collett family who used the premises as a bakery. The water-wheel has not ground flour since that time. In fact, for several decades earlier a steam-engine kept the grist-mill running for the times when water was insufficent (hence the brick chimney-stack). The wheel will run smoothly again, when the bearing and cogs are restored and organically-grown wheat will be ground, and the mill's future secured for new generations through the enterprise of Nicholas Grainger and Gerald Harris.

All six walks in this guide begin as from the door of the Old Mill in Lower Slaughter.

The footpath enters Hollow Bottom

TOPPING HOLLOW BOTTOM
with short fieldpath stroll option 1.5 miles

WALK ONE 3.6 miles - allow 2¼ hours

Walk left from the Old Mill along Mill Lane. At the junction go left, at the right-hand corner, beside Allotment Cottages, go through the kissing-gates to embark upon the straight passage between horse paddocks, with young hedge to the right. Looking back notice the way aligns with the church spire, strongly suggesting its origins as a church approach. A kissing-gate at the end leads through a mature copse and within a few strides to a gate into a meadow, proceed to the new kissing-gate to join the Wardens' Way. Head through the middle of a long sheep pasture, with shallow ridge-and-furrow and the semi-wild course of the River Eye down to the left. This ever popular path leads to a further kissing-gate, subsequently the handsome

2

WALK ONE
Sketchmap

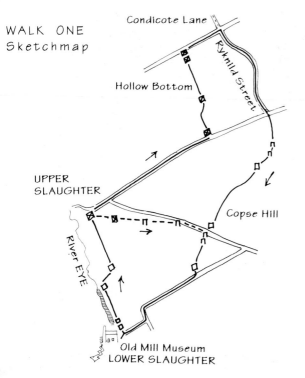

frontage of the Lords of the Manor Hotel, the former Rectory, grace the view beyond the landscaped pond. Bear half right, off the worn path to reach a gate giving access to the minor road.

Strollers seeking to abbreviate their walk should no more than touch the gate diverting smartly right thus following an under-used fieldpath leading east via a gateway (which may be loosely gated). Views of the mature trees that dot and adorn the meadowed vale are a glorious excuse to dawdle and forget time. At the next hedge cross a fence beside a gate, drawing progressively closer to the roadside hedge. Nearing the field corner cross a stile left, onto the road. Go right, where the footpath crosses, take the double-stile right, thus re-uniting with the longer walk.

Go right with the minor road, uphill for 700 yards, till opposite the straight drive to The Old Stables. Go through the field-gate left following the tractor track along the top of the arable field, admire the fine views down upon the Slaughter valley, richly filled with trees. The track switches right through a gate passing along-side a young deciduous planting before bearing down beside the field wall to a frail field-gate (dog leash notice affixed). Descend the bank into Hollow Bottom keeping right in this joyous dell, a sheltered sheep pasture shielded from prevailing winds by a mature beech stand upon the left-hand bank. Pass by Hollow Barn, formerly a sheep and cattle yard, now a stylish house conversion, via a novel swing-latch gate and car park to a gate onto the oft busy B4068. Go right, clinging to the right-hand verge, mindful that there is little warning of swooping traffic. At the top of the rise a cross-roads heralds the arrival of Ryknild Street Roman road.

To the left the ancient road, known as Condicote Lane, runs for two miles across Swell Wold un-metalled. This 'white road' is a reminder of Cotswold highways before the advent of cars and tarmac, an almost unrivalled breezy wold-top 'there and back' walk.

Go right, a thin layer of tarmac poorly disguising the white road beneath.

Condicote Lane

In late spring May blossom gives the walker a special pleasure beside the flanking drystone walls. The way strangely twists off the Roman course, only to regain it short of the junction. Go straight across, with a wall to the right, the views are eastward to Stow-on-the-Wold and beyond the Maugersbury Gap, Icomb and Wyck Beacons. Passing via a broad wall gap the track reduces to a field edge path on descending to a stile.

4

Sunken path leading to St Peter's, Upper Slaughter

Cross The Old Stables and Copse Hill approach carriage-way to a second stile, thus winding on a pleasing path through light woodland, guided by waymarks to a metal kissing-gate. Entering a sloping parkland descend, initially upon the shelving green-way, towards Copse Hill house, then down beside the wooden fence to a kissing-gate at the bottom corner leading onto the road. Meeting up with the short-cut option.

Cross the facing double-stile with a Cotswold Stud notice, the path leads in 15 yards to a stile entry to a broad pasture beset with buttercups and faint traces of ridge-and-furrow cultivation. Traverse diagonally to a white kissing-gate into the tall stand of trees leading to a final kissing-gate onto the road. Go right to complete the walk along Allotment Furlong, passing the entrance to 'Slaughters United Cricket Club'.

SLAUGHTER VALE

A casual stroll around the villages
of Upper and Lower Slaughter.

WALK TWO   2.9 miles - allow 2 hours

SEE CENTRE-SPREAD FOR ROUTE MAP

From the Mill go left and left again accompanying the Wardens' Way via two kissing-gates and thus beside the placid waters of the millstream.   A kissing-gate heralds sheep pasture lined with shallow ridge-and-furrow, bear half-right to a new kissing-gate then walk through the middle of the next pasture with the natural waters edge below.   At a kissing-gate the scene gains a distinctly parkland feel, take the indistinct path bearing half right to a gate onto the road.   Go left down the hill, just short of the road bridge, divert right, passing beyond the seat to clamber over the unnecessarily high-stepped stile. Until the 1930s there was a circular Sheepwash located at this spot, the cottage overlooking the scene 'The Bridges', refers to the sluice bridge (now gone), which spanned the stream adjacent to the stile. The footpath runs through this vestige marsh (original 'slough') with waters running on either hand to a stile, do not cross the footbridge beside the picturesque ford, instead continue upstream to the simple stone bridge infront of Cambray's Farm.

Join the track, going right beneath a canopy of trees inhibiting the drying out of the surface after rain giving a proplencity to muddy conditions.   From a gate the track pursues an open course rising up a sheep pasture to a bridle-gate. Continue to a gate beside Cress Cottage, but for the bridleway, a secluded retreat perched above the wooded dell.   Join the track which runs on a declining course down the woodland banks by a pond and beside the merry waters of the juvenile River Eye.   Strollers may deem it sufficient to cease their advance at the recessed cattle-grid entry to Swiss Farm, pause awhile and admire the setting, surely this is one of the most beautifully situated houses in the Cotswolds.

The millstream, Lower Slaughter

Backtrack beyond Cress Cottage, down the sheep pasture track to the gate. Branch right over the stone stile, after a few yards, clambering diagonally left up the wooded bank on a simple path (no facilitating steps here). From the stile at the top proceed with the wall to the left down to a gate onto the road, go left at the junction down the footway of the village street and left again at The Square. The cottages to the right, on entry to St Peter's were re-modelled by Sir Edwin Lutyens, whilst the farmyard across the way, with new holiday cottage barn conversions rests upon the site of a thirteenth-century late Norman motte. The sunken path leads directly to the church door, look within, then as you come out turn left down the path to a wicket-gate onto the street with the old village school imme-diately to the left. Go either left down the hill and back upon the marsh path or right passing the entry to the gracious Lords of the Manor Hotel, former Rectory.

Lords of the Manor Hotel

The roadway curves left, seek the Wardens' Way sign directing right down a footpath passage to the little clapper bridge over the infant Eye. From the ensuing kissing-gate ascend to retrace your approach via the next two kissing-gates, then bear half left to a gate through the mature spinney and subsequent kissing-gate. Proceed along the fenced passage between horse paddocks walking with the spire of Lower Slaughter church directly ahead, pass through an enclosure via kissing-gates onto the road.

St Mary's, Lower Slaughter

Go forward to the next corner where the Hatch Patch conservation garden should be inspected (information board). Look beyond to the gabled cottage-like dove-cote, the doves originally providing a source of fresh meat for the Manor during winter months, when otherwise only salted meat was available. Go right along the footway to visit the church, the top of the spire incidentally is made of fibre-glass! Go right at the road-bridge before the Washbourne Court Hotel, noted for its cuisine, proceed along the roadway by the triangular Square, pleasingly flanked by cottages. A passage path makes an alternative return approach to the Old Mill, or simply parade by the water's edge, with ducks to charm your steps. Incidentally, the river-name Eye, derives from the Old English 'ea' meaning 'water'.

Washbourne Court Hotel

BAKERY ON THE HILL

WALK THREE 2.7 miles - allow 1½ hours

Leave the Mill left and immediately left, footpath sign Wardens' Way. A passage leading between the Mill and Millstream Cottage via successive kissing-gates, the last a village commemoration of the wedding on 29 July 1981 of Prince Charles and Lady Diana Spencer. The footpath runs alongside the millstream with horse paddock fencing right. At a kissing-gate the path bears half right to a new kissing-gate then along the middle of the next sheep pasture to a kissing-gate thereafter, with pleasing parkland views across the pond to the Lords of the Manor Hotel. Descend to a kissing-gate and low bridge over the River Eye, a confined path rises to the road in Upper Slaughter. Go left passing The Square, *a sunken path gives access to St Peter's.*

Cottage row in Upper Slaughter

10

WALK   THREE
   Sketchmap

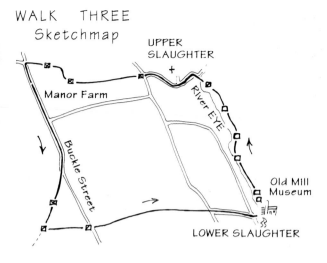

Continue   up
the   footway,
beyond the car
park entry to
the   Lords   of
the Manor Ho-
tel, at the junc-
tion go forward
through   the
wooden   gate
and   into   the
initially sunken
bridleway, with
allotment gar-
dens right. The
way runs   up
sheep pastures to a galvanised gate right, thereafter
an open track swinging round to a gate into a lane leads
by cottages to the road.   Go left upon the road,
passing the new spacious premises of Collett's Bakery:
without question *the finest bread in the Cotswolds*, it
has operated from amongst the former farm-buildings
of Manor Farm only since 1994.   The gable-date 1910
and letter 'B' confirms when the Manor Farm was
established here by the Brassey family, from the vicin-
ity of Upper Slaughter Manor.   So the move of the
bakery business is just another natural switch from
the valley to the wold.

   The road is known as Buckle Street the name has
Saxon not Roman origins, 'Buckle' refers to a certain
landowning lady Burghild, who lived in the Vale of
Evesham, where this old trading route stems. Ignoring
the minor road left, branch right 350 yards beyond
where a bridle-lane forks.   Proceed on this fine way,
enjoying the wonderfully panoramic views across the
Windrush valley towards Cold Aston, via a gate and 100
yards short of the next gate, go left at the galvanised
bridle-gate.   Traverse an arable field (little hampered
by cropping, due to regular use) to a bridle-gate.   Cross
Buckle Street following the bridle-lane over the ridge
and on down the by-road into Lower Slaughter.

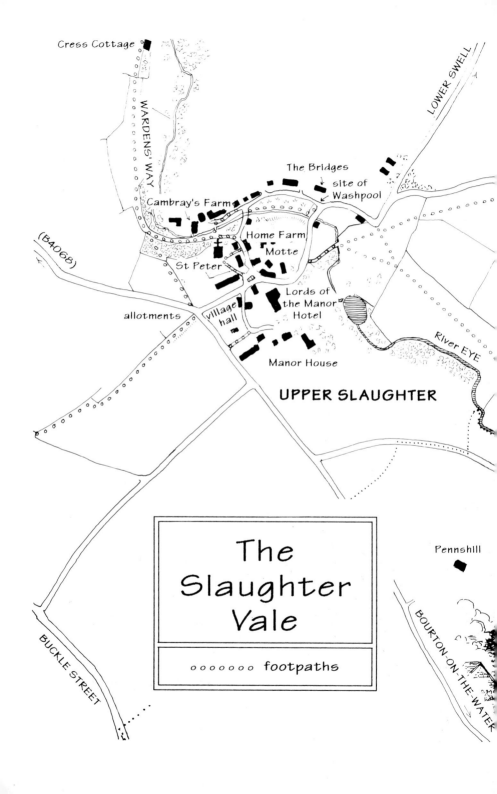

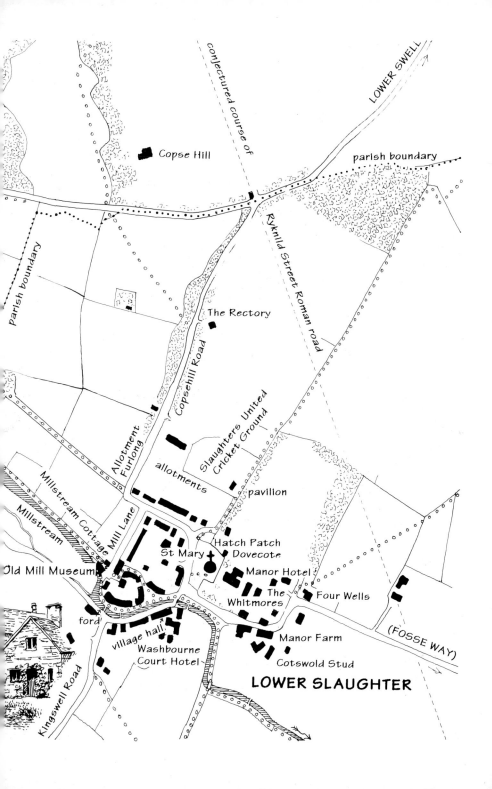

LOWER SLAUGHTER

BOURTON-ON-THE-WATER
WALK FOUR 3.6 miles - allow 2½ hours

Walk right from the Mill along the footway beside the millstream confluence with the River Eye crossing the first stone footbridge.   Go left then right up the minor road rising out of the village to a junction.   Cross straight over into the bridle-lane.   Cresting the ridge cross the minor road to a bridle-gate, traverse the arable field to another galvanised bridle-gate.   Go left down the track via a gate to enter a confined lane leading down to a track junction.   A right-hand turn brings Aston Mill into view.   However, the walk actually goes left along the woodland fringe to briefly join the tree colonised railway track-bed, then bears off right to a bridle gate.   Proceed with the fence to a bridle-gate into a sheep pasture maintaining course to reach the banks of the River Windrush and then the stile/gate onto the Fosse Way at Bourton Bridge.   Caution needed in crossing the main road, taking a glance at the fine bridge, a Roman bridge once spanned the river here, the present structure dates from 1806 (widened in 1959).

Bourton Bridge

14

WALK FOUR
Sketchmap

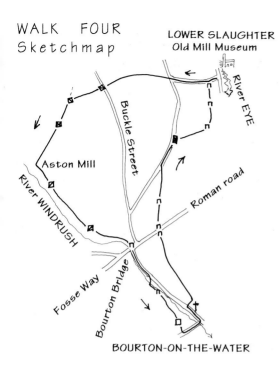

LOWER SLAUGHTER
Old Mill Museum

River EYE

Buckle Street

Aston Mill

River WINDRUSH

Roman road

Fosse Way

Bourton Bridge

BOURTON-ON-THE-WATER

Follow the footway into Bourton-on-the-Water beside the river fringed with pollarded willow. At 'Strathspey' B&B go right along the confined footpath tight by the wall and beneath trees to cross a stone footbridge with its fine view of Lansdown Mill House. Follow the true right bank, initially with water on both sides 'Mesopatamian fashion', to a wicket kissing-gate. After an old hedge line the path bears away from the river's edge to a metal kissing-gate. A confined path leads into the side street, with Harrington House opposite; architecturally the finest house in the village, revered by a steady stream of HF walkers.

Go left to cross the Windrush, admiring the sequence of 'Venetian' bridges and the Motor Museum (former corn mill) left. At the junction go left and after the fish & chip shop go right up the path by St Lawrence's church with distinctive dome and fine interior. At the cross-paths go left following the path beyond the primary school which becomes confined, cross the railway embankment traversing the field to a stile/gate onto the Fosse Way. Again cross carefully, to a double stile in the tall cypress hedge. Ascend the arable field to a footbridge and stone slab stile. Bear half right up the pasture to gain the minor road, go right. After 300 yards go right at a gate, descend the pasture upon a bridleway keeping the hedge to the left. Near the foot

15

go left, over the stile, following a footpath aiming for the first pole to avoid the wet ground and reach a stile into a small field the path continues to a stile onto the road to complete the walk.

IN SEARCH
OF THE DIKLER

WALK FIVE   2.2 miles - allow 1¼ hours

Walk right from the Old Mill along the initially narrow path beside the outflowing mill stream. The path accompanies the gliding River Eye along the village street, alive with ducks, admire the charming foot-bridges to reach the road bridge, opposite Washbourne Court Hotel. Cross directly over following the footway downstream, at hand the roadside verge, the normal short-stay parking place of visitors. Keep company with the stream beyond the weir as it bends right (Wardens' Way signpost), opposite the entrance to Lower Slaughter Manor Hotel.

Lower Slaughter Manor Hotel

16

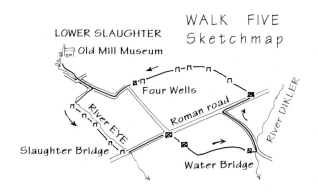

LOWER SLAUGHTER
Old Mill Museum
Four Wells
River EYE
Roman road
River DIKLER
Slaughter Bridge
Water Bridge

Here the stream's character changes; the wall retaining banks giving way to a gravel-bedded more natural overhung watercourse. Where the river bends left, leave the popular path continuing downstream from the stile along a footpath marshalled by fencing to the right. The path keeps company with the river via stiles to reach Slaughter Bridge and the Fosse Way. This was the junction of two Roman roads, with Ryknild Street converging from a north-westerly direction.

Cross the road, going left, after 350 yards go right. At Pike Cottage divert right through the gate into a bridle-lane the bridleway is confined via gates to the crossing of the Dikler bridle-bridge. Reaching the minor road go left past Snipe Moss, the Bourton Vale Equine Clinic and Greenfingers B&B, to the Fosse Way junction, go right upon the footway to its conclusion by Gilders Transport yard and opposite Lakeside B&B.

Cross gingerly to a gate/footpath sign, keep left along the edge of the arable land to a stile at a corner left, keeping the hedge to the right, continue via a foot-bridge and three stiles, latterly crossing a broad pasture to a stile beside Four Wells house. Pass through the garden discreetly to a white wicket-gate onto the drive, go left to gain the road by the entrance to The Whitmores private estate; derived from the family name of the former lords of the manor.

Follow the road back into the village.

STOW-ON-THE-WOLD

WALK SIX 8.6 miles - allow 4 hours

From the Old Mill go left along Mill Lane bear right, then at the right bend, go left by the Hatch Patch wildlife conservation garden. A footpath signpost, with a Heart of England Way waymark, guides between the new houses and passage to a wicket-gate appropriately entering the cricket enclosure behind the pavilion. Continue alongside the woodland strip to exit via a stile. Passing via a tall hedge gap aligned with the old ridge-and-furrow to reach a gate in the tall hedge to the right. Go left, a wide green margin affording comfortable walking alongside arable land, giving a pleasing view back to Lower Slaughter Manor Hotel. The path bears right to a simple plank footbridge, then slants half-left to a gate, and target waymarker. From this spot the quiet pastoral vale dotted with trees is a special delight.

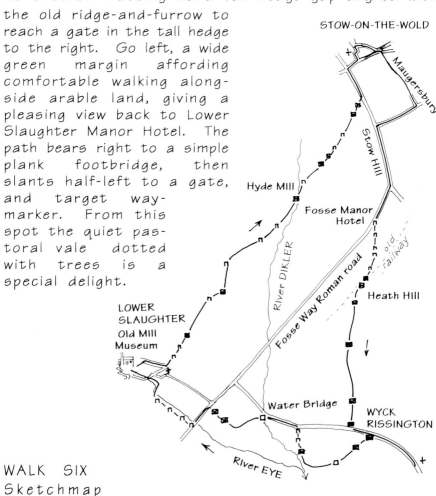

STOW-ON-THE-WOLD

Maugersbury

Stow Hill

Hyde Mill

Fosse Manor Hotel

River DIKLER

old railway

Fosse Way Roman road

Heath Hill

LOWER SLAUGHTER
Old Mill
Museum

Water Bridge

WYCK RISSINGTON

River EYE

WALK SIX
Sketchmap

The footpath traverses the ensuing pasture to a novel squeeze stile affixed to a field-gate, where footpaths intersect. A signpost directs right to 'Hide Mill', cross the cattle pasture to a further squeeze stile/gate. Bear left through the ditch gap then half right with a conservation pond filled with bull-rushes over to the right, to a further ditch passage stile/gate. Half left to final squeeze stile/gate then continue forward in pasture to a stile close by the River Dikler. Notice the charming clapper bridge in the grounds of Hyde Mill. The path leads on through a water meadow to a galvanised kissing-gate. Go right over the little bridge upon the track to Hyde Mill ('hide' being a Saxon measure of land approximating to 120 acres). Bear left past the cottage and over the access bridge spanning the mill-stream, a beautiful spot to pause and gaze particularly upstream. Notice the long out-dated sign 'Bridle Road Stow Station'; the railway closed in 1964!

Delightful view from the lane to Quarwood Cottage

Take the footpath left signed 'Public Footpath Stow-on-the Wold' via a stile, traverse the pasture, with Nether Swell Manor attractively set up to the left, notice the inverted 'S' alignment of the ridge-and-furrow indicative of oxen ploughing. Pass to the left of the poultry housing to a stile beyond a cattle trough. Go forward via the stile ascending the access drive by The Unicorn Hotel's Carriage Driving Team stables. Crossing the drive to Nether Swell Manor, rising on past more stables via double-gates to enter the wooded bank at a hand-gate. A short climb, slanting right beneath a fox earth, leads to a stile into sheep pasture completing the ascent, note the fine view left upon Lower Swell, to a gate into a lane.

The lane leads pleasantly via two further gates, past the crazy paving-style masonry of Quarwood Cottage to reach the Fosse Way. Cross with the utmost care to the footway on the far side, Go left up Stow Hill, to enter the 'wold-top' village of Stow-on-the-Wold.

Digbeth Street leading down from The Square

Ascend to the traffic lights go right along Sheep

Street then left by Church Street, perhaps glancing aside to view the church before entering the bustling Square. Bear right, down Digbeth Street and Park Street, going right at the fork by 'The Bell' embarking upon the Maugersbury Park avenue with the public conveniences and car park to the left. What a joy to stroll back into quiet countryside down this delightful embowered old carriageway. The drive leads past Maugersbury Manor down to a crossways, go right along the truncated road with fine views across the Maugersbury Gap to Icomb Beacon. The road is beginning to show the signs of neglect and minor subsidence is causing lateral cracks to appear. Near the end a new house basks in a marvellous vista of the Evenlode vale, which runs from the distant Chipping Norton via Churchill and the Cornbury vestige of Wychwood Forest.

Regaining the Fosse Way go left downhill, the junction traffic islands and lights are some assistance to a

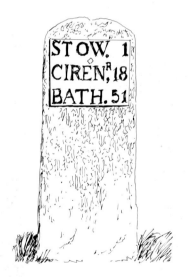

Fosse Way milestone

safe crossing, firstly to the greatly enlarged former Farmers Arms (now Farmers Lodge), after the old milestone (its destinations confirming the Fosse Way's Roman credentials) cross to the verge leading on past the Fosse Manor Hotel. Subsequently cross the main road once more to the parking area where a footpath sign directs via a stile into a large pasture field. Cross diagonally right to a stile in the corner, walk alongside the old railway fencing to a gate left where cross the old Kingham Junction to Cheltenham line, now host to conifers at this point.

From the ensuing stile go right keeping beside the tall hedge until it makes a modest swerve, here slant half left across the pasture to the bushes, proceeding to a stile in the field corner, keeping the hedge to the left. Go left on the green track, bear right, not directly into the farmyard, to double-gates, join the Heath Hill farm track going right at the broad area beyond the cottages leave the drive left by the double-gates angling half right across the pasture, oft grazed by a herd of Ayrshire cows, to a gate. Now pursue the left-hand hedge to wooden double-gates, cross the next pasture to corresponding twin-gates to join the road, go left.

The Oxfordshire Way bridleway departs from the road right, immediately prior to the open green. However, make time to stroll the length of this beautiful village street to admire St Laurence's Church, where Gustav Holst experienced his first professional engagement as organist, at the age of seventeen, in 1892-3.

Return to the double-gates and follow the green way via further double-gates, shortly after guided right to a railed stream bridge via gates. The green-way runs clear course beyond, divert from this 100 yards short of the Dikler bridle-bridge, walking upstream via a gate seeking a stile/gate left into a 60 yard fenced passage to a gate, continue with the hedge to the right via a gate and subsequent stile onto the road, go left. Crossing the old railway road-bridge divert left with the bridleway which crosses the Dikler at Water Bridge. Continuing confined via gates to reach the Fosse Way at Pike Cottage. Follow the foot-way left for 350 yards to Slaughter Bridge where cross the main road and follow the stiled path beside the River Eye back into Lower Slaughter.

A serene scene, the ford at Upper Slaughter

Footbridge over the River Eye in Lower Slaughter

The Cotswold Way

If you have enjoyed the walks in this guide, then perhaps you might like to set about tackling the region's 'big walk', the COTSWOLD WAY.

One hundred miles of deliciously diverse scenery running the entire length of the Cotswold escarpment, up hill, down dale, from the quintessential Cotswold town of Chipping Campden to the gracious city of Bath.

Let the miles fall away at your feet, roll down the pages of time and tide at your own comfortable pace, steadily piecing the route together. So that, in the fullness of time, you may know the secrets of the Cotswold Edge, the quiet beauty of leafy lanes and village paths, of scarp and woodland ways, a bounty to enjoy through all, or any season.

For the best and most up-to-date guidance to the route, get the **WALKABOUT** series guide written by *Mark Richards*.

It is widely obtainable within the Cotswold region, or direct from :

REARDON Publishing,
56 Upper Norwood Street,
Leckhampton,
CHELTENHAM,
Glos GL53 0DU

Please send a large stamped (2 X First Class) addressed envelope for our free illustrated booklist and mail order details